PATRICIA
MORRIS

The Piccolo Study Book

NOVELLO PUBLISHING LIMITED

CONTENTS

In memory of William Morris

Exclusive distributors:
Hal leonard Europe Limited
42 Wigmore Street
Marylebone, London, W1U 2RN
All rights reserved.

Order No. NOV120829
ISBN 0-85360-852-0
© Copyright 1998 Novello & Company Limited,
14/15 Berners Street, London W1T 3LJ.

Music processed by Stave Origination.
Book design by Pearce Marchbank, Studio Twenty.
Printed in the United Kingdom by
Caligraving Limited, Thetford, Norfolk.

PREFACE

I have often been asked about the process of warming up and practising the piccolo. Most flute players these days need to be able to play the piccolo. The telephone rings and it is too late to do enough basic practice to feel secure in the concert. I hope that this book of warm up exercises and studies will enable flautists to 'keep their lip in' on the piccolo: then it is fun to play in the orchestra. Once you have addressed the minor adjustments necessary to transfer your flute embouchure to the piccolo, a regular input of 30 to 40 minutes a day should enable you to gain the same security and expressive qualities as you possess on the flute.

The piccolo is essentially an orchestral instrument so your practise schedule will certainly need to reflect the techniques required for the repertoire. For example, long *piano* notes for Shostakovich symphonies; a secure, *pianissimo* top register for Beethoven's Symphony No.9; fast articulation in Rimsky-Korsakov's Sheherazade; *forte* low register solos in Ravel's G Major Piano Concerto.

The studies in this book are grouped into sections dealing with specific technical areas; by working through them as part of your regular practice routine you will acquire the technique required for orchestral playing. Some studies have been transposed and some have dynamics and articulation altered to help develop this expertise.

Patricia Morris

WARMING UP

The most important adjustment to make when playing the piccolo is the increase in air speed and support for the breath. The embouchure hole is too small to allow huge quantities of air, and if you are to avoid tiring the embouchure, the air speed needs to be very fast. You are, after all, playing one octave higher than on the flute.

One way to gain this extra support from the diaphragm is to take in a reasonable breath and imagine you are trying to blow up a new balloon. This should result in a maintained tension between the diaphragm and the intercostal muscles which will produce the required air speed for the piccolo.

Before you begin these warm-up exercises, tune your piccolo – always practise with the headjoint pulled out the correct amount. One of the difficulties of the piccolo is training the embouchure to make very small adjustments – much smaller than for the flute. To be certain of the pitch you will produce, start by playing single semibreves, beginning in the middle register and listening hard to make sure the pitch is always exactly the same. Pull the instrument away and try again – remembering the pitch. Practising this exercise without the tongue ensures a more careful placement of embouchure and support. Try extending the final note to at least 30-40 seconds, *piano*. This is long enough for all Shostakovich symphonies, Prokofiev's Romeo and Juliet and Bartók's Concerto For Orchestra.

Now tune the octaves:

Then, with a full warm sound, play the exercise below, listening to the pitch of the tonic and making sure you return to it exactly. Check the intonation of the fifths.

Continue the exercise by transposing down a semitone each time:

...as far as you can, until you reach the key of G. Then practise in ascending keys, beginning on middle F♯ and transposing up a semitone each time. By starting your practice routine with these exercises, the little muscles in the centre of your embouchure will learn where to place themselves.

You will almost certainly by now (if not earlier) need to relax the lips. Whistle tones and playing harmonics are excellent for this. Sometimes it is refreshing to return to the flute to play harmonics.

Now, to place the embouchure for the upper register, with a *piano* dynamic. It is very important to maintain the breath support and to observe the dynamics in the following exercise. If the third note is sharp enough, *pianissimo* and the air speed fast, the top note will come out *pianissimo* with no further effort:

Play this in all possible keys, ascending from middle D.

If you consider where the note sounds rather than where it is written, it will help you to provide the proper support. Play the following extract on the flute an octave up, and then on the piccolo as written.

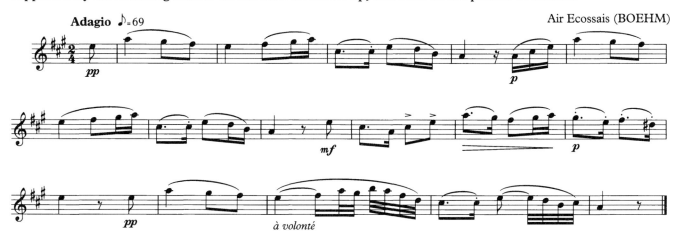

There are many tunes you can experiment with in this way, including the Poulenc Flute Sonata, the Telemann Fantasias and C.P.E. Bach's A Minor Sonata for unaccompanied flute. Try any slow movements from Baroque sonatas, shaping the phrases as you would on the flute; take care that the upper notes have the same resonance and dynamic as the lower. The extra brightness of the sound often begins from middle B upwards. Remember your success with the triplet exercise on the previous page – you have no need to blow louder for the top register.

It is important to acquire this colour and *piano* dynamic for the upper register to enable you to blend in *pianissimo* chords (for example in Mahler symphonies). It is essential that you do not squeeze down on the embouchure to speed up the air. Try to play on the inside of both lips. The early studies in this book will help you to develop the same colour and dynamic through the registers, provided you listen well.

Just one more tip. It is very easy to tense your shoulders and arms whilst playing the piccolo – avoid this simply by being aware of it. Keep your throat open.

Section 1 - SOUND AND FLEXIBILITY

These studies are arranged progressively so that you gradually increase your flexibility
as you work through them. Practise them slowly enough to keep your tone constant
in its resonance regardless of the octave. The low register should be focussed and
not too sharp, and the top octave shouldn't be too bright in colour.

1.

Moderato, with a full sound

N. PLATONOV

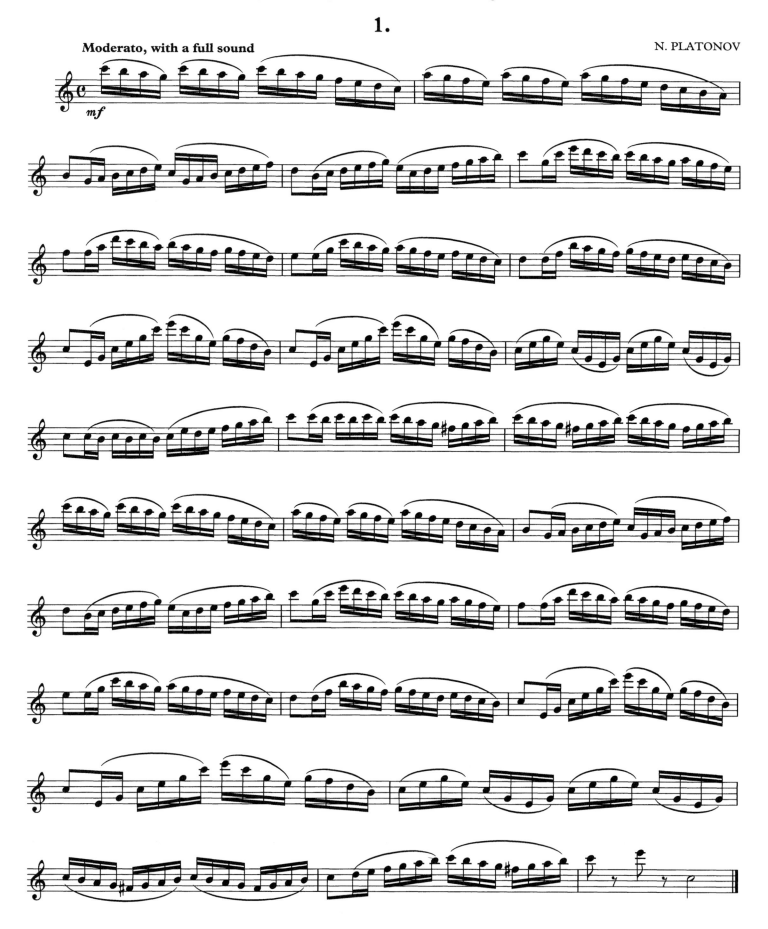

2.

G. GARIBOLDI

3.

This study will help to strengthen the low register, which is naturally weak on the piccolo.
There are plenty of beautiful low register solos in the orchestral repertoire: Ravel's
Mother Goose Suite, Verdi's Requiem and Shostakovich's symphonies,
especially Nos. 5 and 8.

A.B. FÜRSTENAU

10

4.

This study should help you develop the resonances and dynamics needed
for the last movement of Beethoven's Symphony No.9.

V. DE MICHELIS

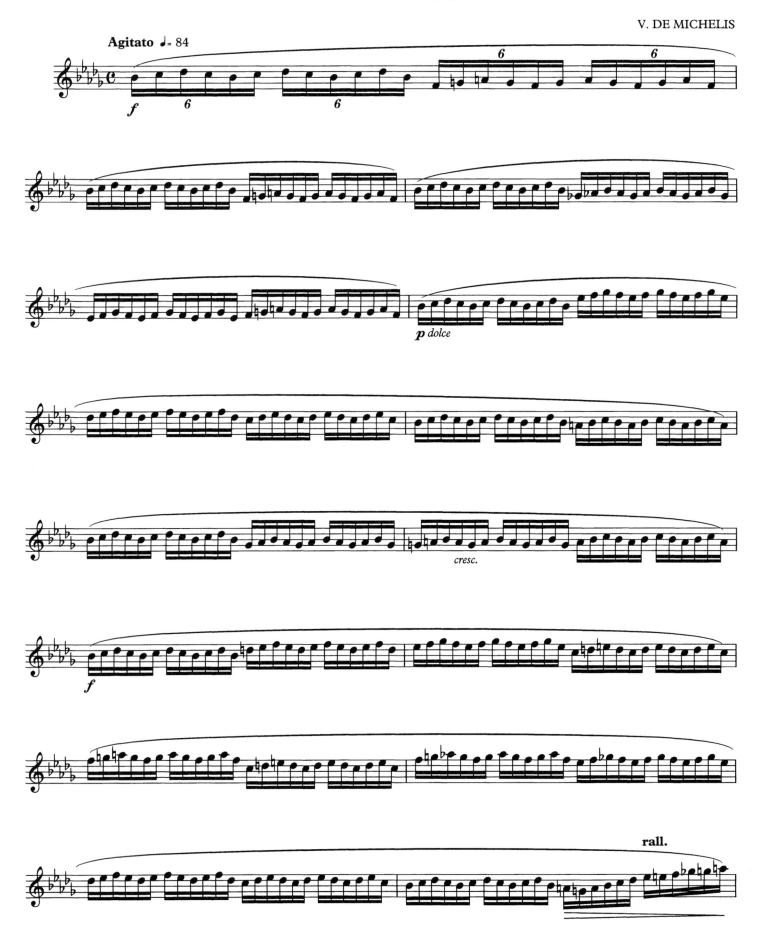

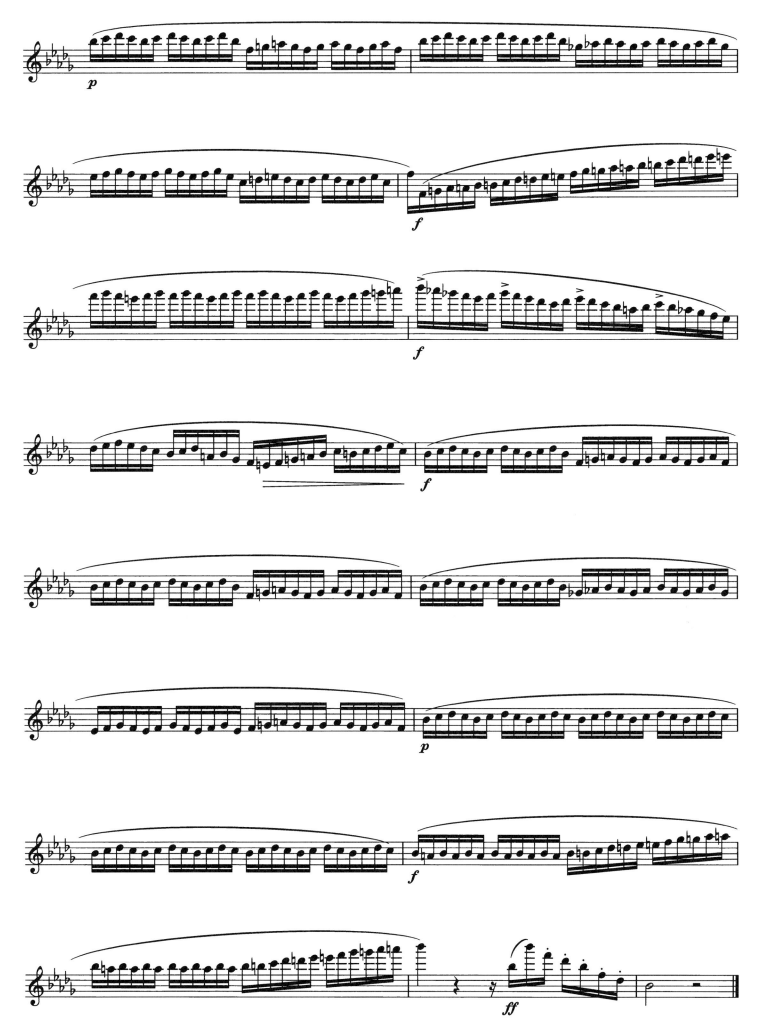

5.

J. ANDERSEN

6.

E. KÖHLER

7.

Play this with a full sound, making sure that the upper of each pair of notes is quieter.
To achieve this, at first slow the study right down and practise like this:

T. BOEHM

Allegretto con moto

8.

J. ANDERSEN

9.

E. KÖHLER

10.

T. BOEHM

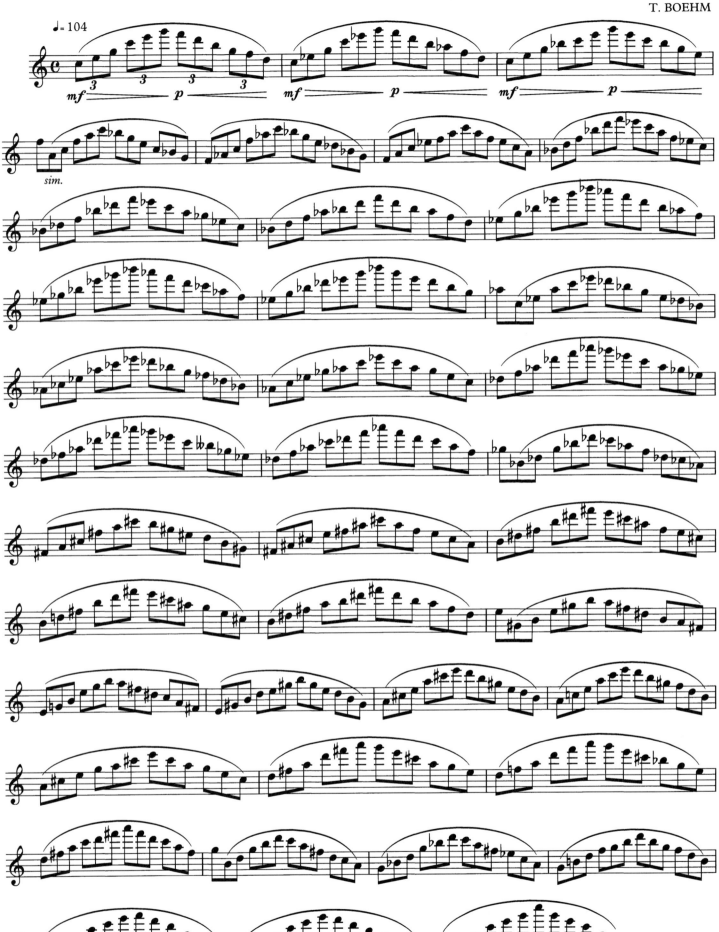

11.

Great care is needed to make sure the upper notes are neither louder nor brighter
than the rest. Developing this balance will be very useful for pieces such as the
3rd movement of Dvořák's Symphony No.6, the 4th movement of Shostakovich's
Symphony No.8 and the 1st movement of Shostakovich's Symphony No.6.

G. BRICCIALDI

Section 2 - ARTICULATION

There are many very fast and exciting piccolo solos which need clear articulation.
It's important to make sure that your sound is focussed and clear - especially in the
lower and middle register. Pay attention to the top lip and make sure it remains
relaxed: imagining a space between the teeth and the top lip often helps. Begin
with single tonguing and work through these studies, gradually increasing the
tempo. You'll find that 'tongue fatigue' goes after a few weeks!

I would also recommend that you practise flutter tonguing - beginning *piano* in the
second register without an explosion is not always easy! A slower roll of the tongue
helps, or if possible use the throat flutter. Make sure the pitch is not too flat. There
are many instances where flutter tonguing is needed in orchestral repertoire
(Stravinsky's The Fairy's Kiss and Shostakovich's Symphony No.4, for example).

12.

Practise this with single tonguing.

T. BOEHM

rit.　　　a tempo

cresc.　　　*f*

f 2nd time *p*

cresc.　　　*sempre stacc.*

f

13.

Practise this study *forte*, then *piano*.

H. SOUSSMANN

Allegro ♩= 120-138 (single tonguing) ♩= 138-152 (double tonguing)

sempre staccato

14.

Practise this firstly *forte*, then *piano*, then with dynamics given.

J. ANDERSEN

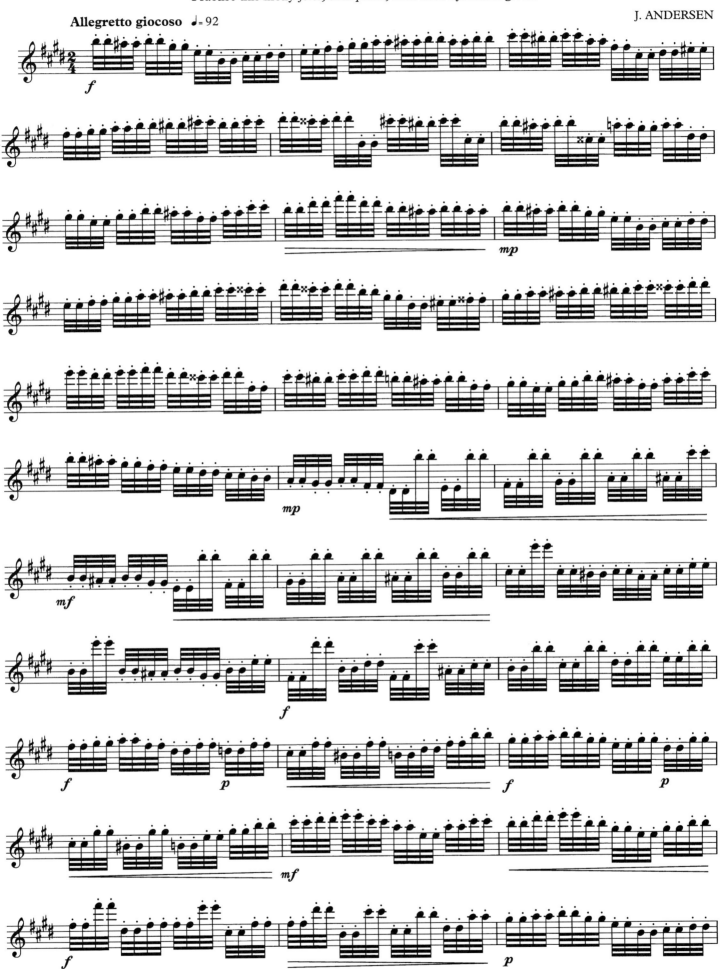

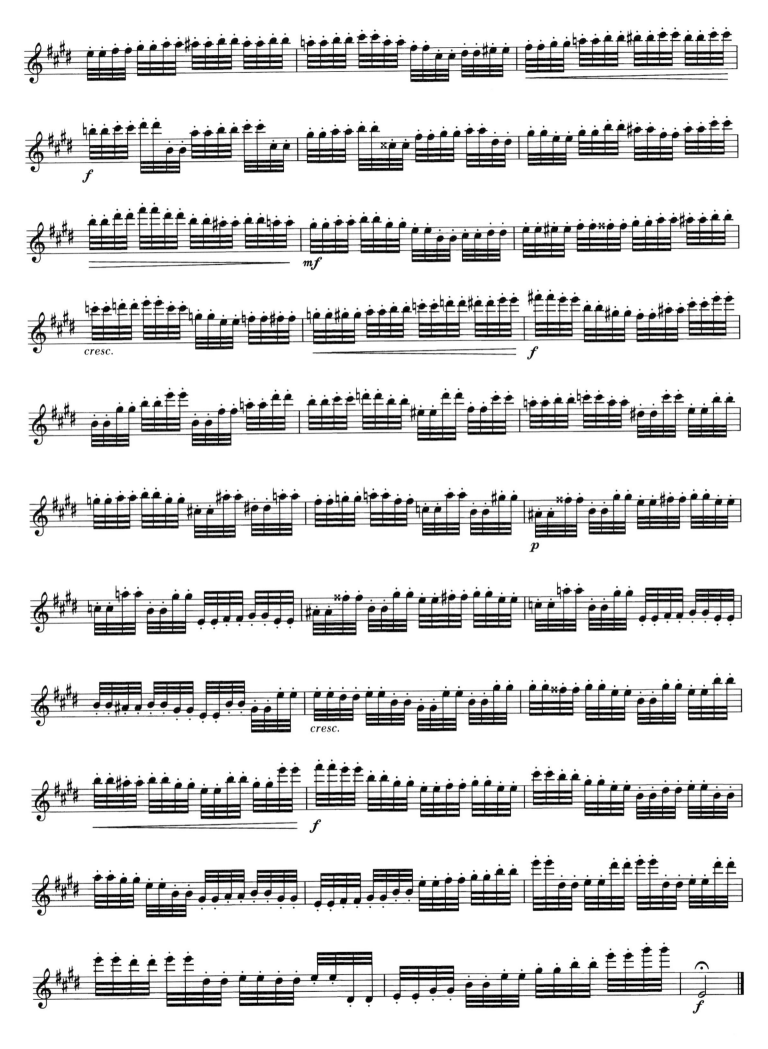

15.

Practise this firstly *forte* and then *piano* throughout. The repeated notes will help you to
increase the speed of your tonguing, preparing you for such pieces as Di Ballo Overture
by Sullivan and the last movement of Sheherazade by Rimsky-Korsakov.

G. GARIBOLDI

16.

Practise this tongued both TKT TKT and TKT KTK. The second version tends
to be less clear, but you can articulate more quickly - a great help in Debussy's La Mer and
Chant du Rossignol by Stravinsky.

H. SOUSSMANN

Più allegro ♩=88-96 (T-K-T, T-K-T) 96-108 (T-K-T, K-T-K)

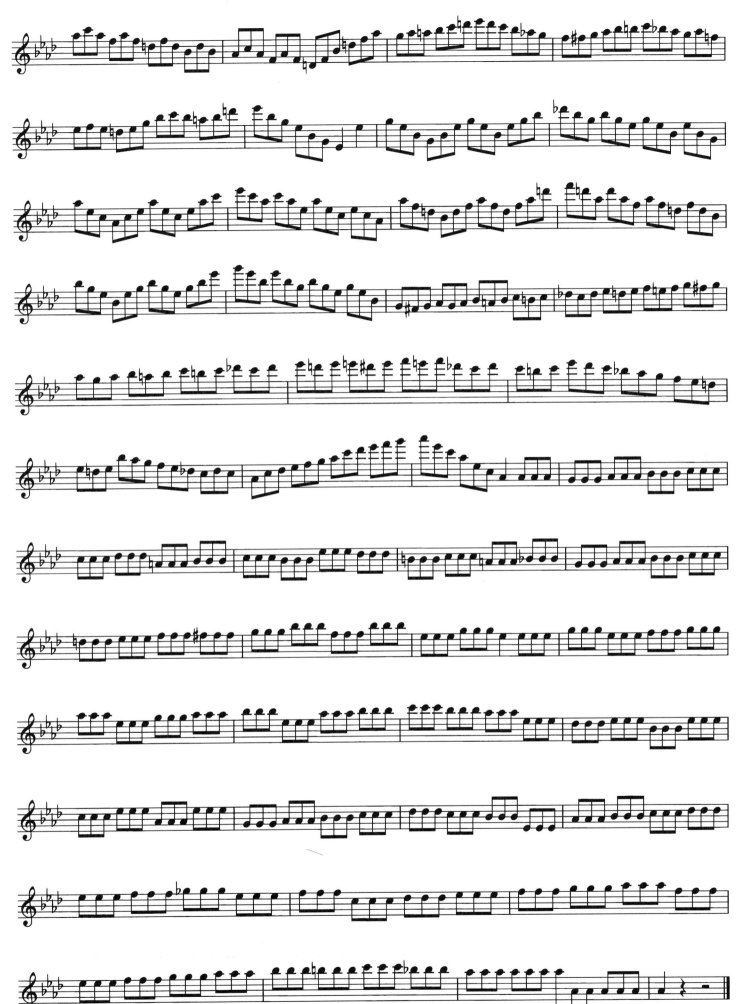

17.

This tricky articulation pattern occurs in many orchestral passages, especially
Rossini's Overtures (Barber of Seville, Journey to Rheims and Seige of Corinth).
Listen carefully – if you cut the second note short it will slow the speed.

L. DORUS

18.

Make sure you play the accents on the lower notes, keep the
articulation light on the second semiquavers and keep it even.

T. BOEHM

19.

Keeping the tonguing light on the second semiquavers - especially with the octave leap -
will be very useful practise for the Vivaldi C major Concerto (1st movement).

Allegro ♩= 120

T. BOEHM

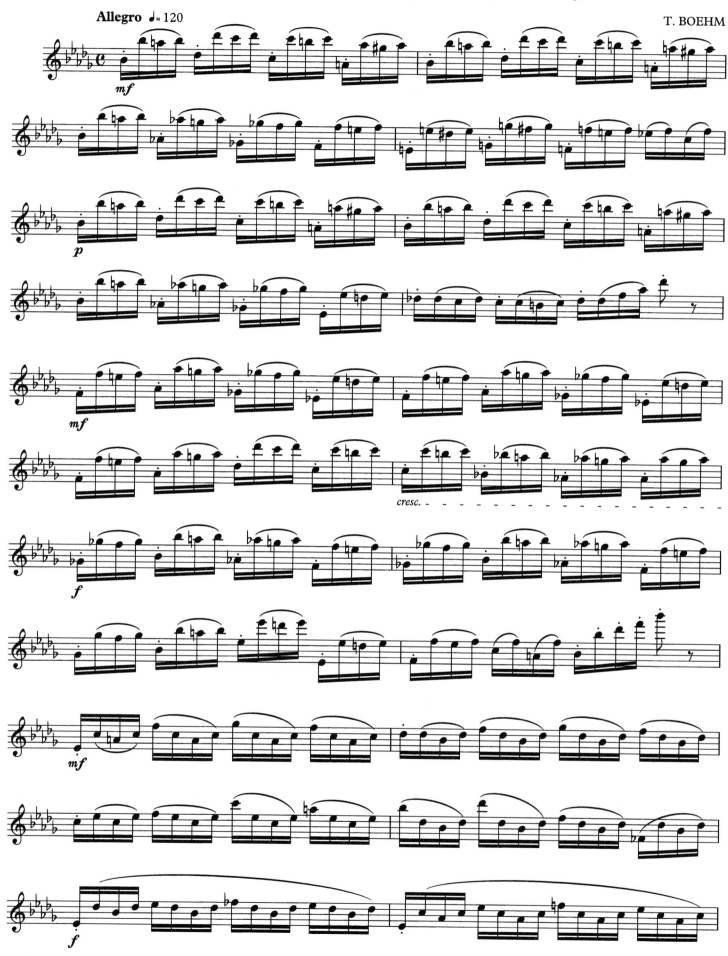

20.

There are many examples in orchestral repertoire where the tempo is too fast for single tonguing: Borodin's Prince Igor Overture and Rimsky-Korsakov's Sheherazade 4th movement, for example. Start by single tonguing this study as fast as you can, and then try using the following articulation:

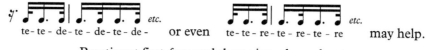

te- te - de - te - de - te - de -   or even   te- te - re - te - re - te - re   may help.

Practise at first *forte* and then *piano* throughout.

H. SOUSSMANN

Section 3 - FINGERING

Because the piccolo does not rest in the cleft of the chin as easily as the flute,
balancing the instrument securely and keeping the fingers independent are
skills you will need to practise. In addition to this, the size and closeness of
the keys will create problems with evenness which you will have to work on.

21.

Practise this exercise in D major and C minor as well.

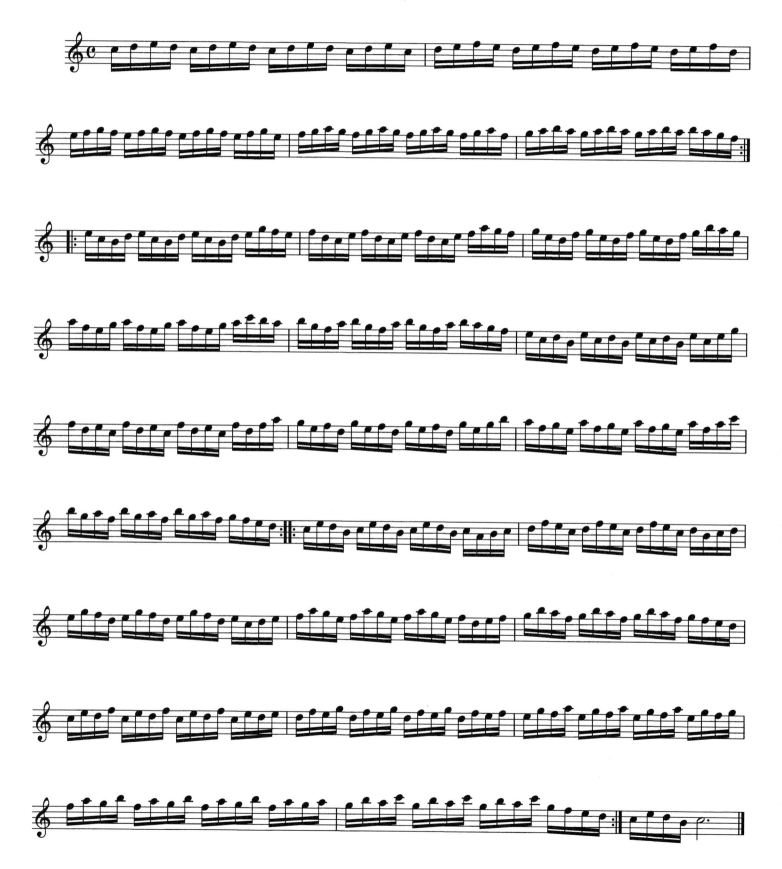

22.

H. SOUSSMANN

44

46

23.

Play this with first finger B♭ fingering.

G. GARIBOLDI

Moderato quasi Andante

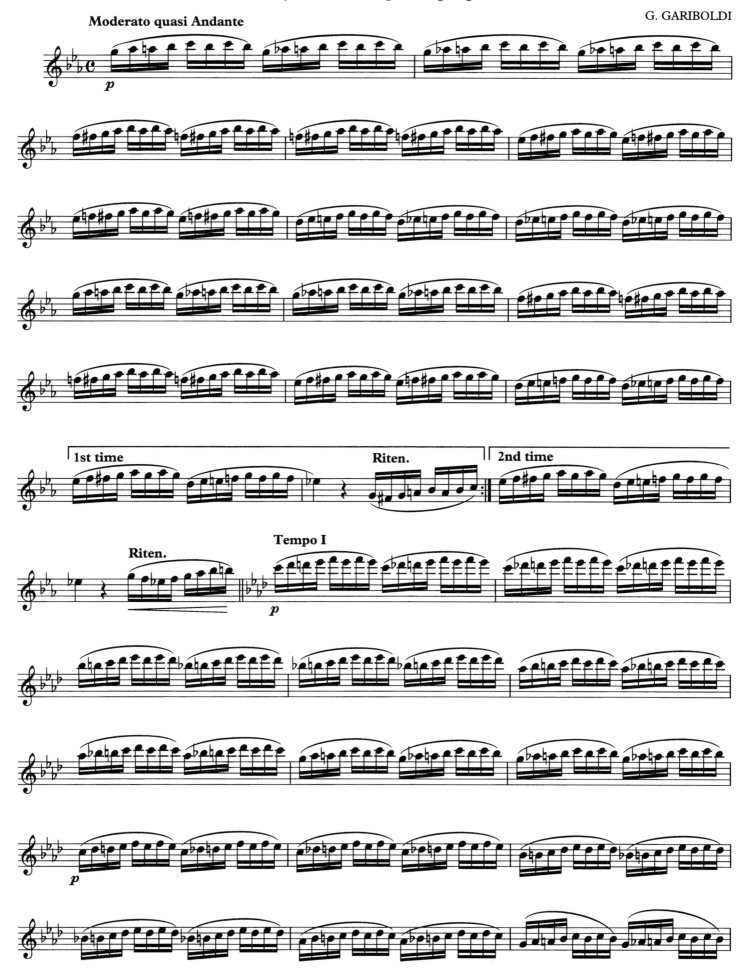

Section 4 - ORNAMENTATION

There are a number of piccolo solos in the orchestral repertoire which require mordents or trills
to be placed on the beat: Bartók's Romanian Dances (Pe Loc) and Witches' Sabbath from
Berlioz's Symphonie Fantastique, for example. This study will help to correct the tendency to put
ornaments before the beat; play each ornament as a mordent of three equal notes on the beat.

24.

Moderato ♩= 84-96

A.B. FÜRSTENAU

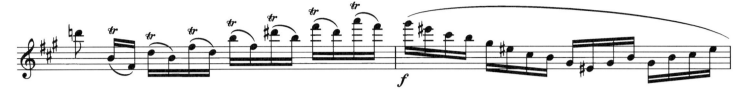

Section 5 - GRANDIOSE STUDIES

As well as being great fun to play, these 'grandiose' studies are excellent for developing
expressive qualities and balancing the resonance of the top and bottom registers.
You should also focus on your intonation - occasional use of a tuning machine
is recommended to make sure your bottom register isn't too sharp.

25.

The construction of the piccolo's scale is often based around tuning the three D♮s,
with each maker deciding on their own compromises. To get the upper D sharp
enough, the middle G and top A are usually sharp. If the middle G is left sharp, the
F♯ (and sometimes F and E) may also be adjusted to even out the discrepancy.

In this study you will need to concentrate on the intonation of the D♮s, which will
help you to learn about your own instrument and adjust accordingly.

A. HUGOT

26.

Be careful of your middle register E♭, which is often very sharp. Check that the little finger key doesn't open too far. You will probably also need to use the following fingering for top A♭:

Con espressione

A.B. FÜRSTENAU

SPECIAL FINGERINGS

These special fingerings are included to help with *pianissimo* long notes – most are very sharp but worth learning because they rarely drop down to the lower register.

First practise each note *mezzo forte* with the normal fingering, then *pianissimo* using the fake fingering. Find where to place the pitch – a tuning machine is helpful. The usefulness of the fingering varies with the make of your instrument. You must learn the fingers you decide to adopt so that they are as familiar to you as the normal fingering. To raise the pitch a small amount on middle A, A♯ and B♮, add the G♯ key.

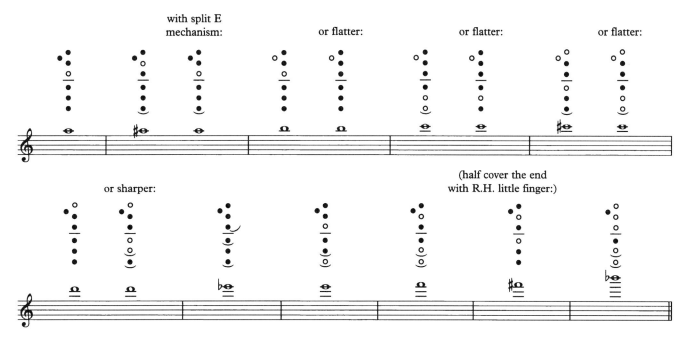

The top register is notoriously difficult to play *piano*. Try this trick: with the right hand little finger, half cover, or sometimes almost totally cover, the end of the piccolo. This helps to remove some resistance and free the sound. It also sharpens most notes on most instruments.

Some flatter fingerings for *fortissimo* tutti notes:

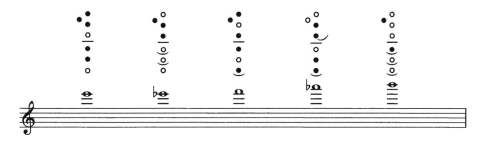

BY PATRICIA MORRIS & TREVOR WYE

Covering all aspects of orchestral playing, these volumes explore repertoire in a unique way, offering the serious student an opportunity to obtain an extensive knowledge of orchestral repertoire.

THE ORCHESTRAL FLUTE PRACTICE BOOK 1

This volume looks at Long Solos, the Big Tunes, Articulation Passages, Pianissimo Passages, Low Solos and Mozart and Haydn, as well as containing many more pages of standard orchestral repertoire (composers A to P). Key comments and hints are included throughout from the extensive orchestral experience of Trevor Wye and Patricia Morris.

NOV120801

THE ORCHESTRAL FLUTE PRACTICE BOOK 2

This volume looks at the Middle and Upper Registers, Cadenzas, Orchestral Duets and Trios, the Austro-German School and Contemporary Orchestral Writing, as well as containing many more pages of standard orchestral repertoire (composers R to Z). Key comments and hints are included throughout from the extensive orchestral experience of Trevor Wye and Patricia Morris.

NOV120802

THE PICCOLO PRACTICE BOOK

This excellent and comprehensive book is designed to help flautists transfer their playing skills to the piccolo by organising the various aspects of technique into a logical sequence through orchestral extracts. It also includes useful information about practising, auditions and buying a piccolo.

NOV120658

THE ALTO FLUTE PRACTICE BOOK

This much awaited book will be of use to students and professionals alike: the first of its kind covering all aspects of the alto flute. Complete with historical notes, useful technical information and a comprehensive repertoire list as well as all the standard orchestral extracts. Information is also given on the bass flute, flute d'amour and contra-alto and contra-bass flutes.

NOV120781

Novello Publishing Limited